BRINGING *SEXY* BACK TO YOUR MARRIAGE

BRINGING *SEXY* BACK TO YOUR MARRIAGE

A Guide To:

Self Satisfaction – Self Realization – Couples Intimacy

GAIL CROWDER

G.A.I.L.
PUBLISHING

Disclaimer: Certain suggestions are made in this book. While these are intended to be helpful to the reader, the reader must assume all risk associated with following any particular suggestion. Therefore, in purchasing this book, the reader agrees that the authors and publisher are not liable or responsible for any injury or damage caused by the use of any information contained herein.

For information contact;
www.gailcrowderinc.com

Book and Cover design by Jen Welzel Designs
Editing by Dieneke Johnson

ISBN: 978-0-9832185-2-4
First Edition: May 2014

10 9 8 7 6 5 4 3 2 1

Reviews

"I absolutely loved the "Bringing the Sexy Back to the Marriage Conference" because it reminded me of my responsibilities as a wife. Instead of focusing on our mate and what they could do for us, it taught me how to work on what I need to do for my marriage. The atmosphere during the conference was a sisterhood among wives I have never experienced. I learned through sharing and an open mind and when I tell you they brought it to us, the conference is a must for any woman engaged or married woman who wants to give and do their best in making sure they live a successful and blessed union! I won't miss the next one and neither should you!! A++."
-- Lisa Washington

"I can't say enough good things about Bring Sexy Back To The Marriage. This conference truly opened my eyes and showed me that my role in my marriage was to be the most sexy, loving, kind and compassionate wife to my husband. BSB brought all that to life for me in a way that was exciting, intimate and loving. It also showed me that I was not alone in my struggles as a wife and having other wives around to support me made all the difference in the world. My advice to any women who wants to take her marriage to the next level, get to BSB, it will change your marriage!"
-- Kiki Ramsey

Acknowledgements

I would like to thank my Lord and Savior, Jesus Christ, for giving me this creative mind, and for allowing me to walk out this predestined journey. To my husband Gil, my friend, my lover, and my sounding board; I thank you for being the man of God that you were called to be, and for allowing me to be just me. To my two sons, Justin and Joshua; Mommy loves you more than life. To my mother, Sharron J. White; thank you so much for believing in me when I didn't believe in myself, and for helping to finance the dream that lives inside me. I am forever grateful. To my Dad Larry P. White thanks so much for allowing me to talk for hours on the phone with you about my dreams for my business. To my Aunt Clarice B. Jackson; thanks for teaching me your grace and elegance. You are truly timeless.

To my sisters not by birth but by spirit -- Joy, Val, Kim, Judy, DeJaun, Chris, Kiki, Tawawn and Kellie -- thank you for being a pain in my-you-know-what? (Smile) For your prayers, your laughs, your tears, your ideas, your phone calls, your support, your helping hands and your love, I am truly grateful. Thank you, thank you!

To Dieneke Johnson; thank you so much for making me shine on paper; I love you so much.

To sexy and potential wives who purchase this book; I pray that you find a tip or an idea that will enhance and enrich your marriage to take it to the next level.

To all the ladies who work hard at the BSB Conference to ensure that the ladies who attend have a good time! I thank you from the bottom of my heart! God Bless you.

With love,

Contents

He Said She Said
Complaints About Sex

The most common complaints from married couples about their sex lives include:

* The relationship is boring

* He/She isn't interested in sex anymore

* We have sex – on special occasions

* Having a family is just too tiring to have a good sex life

* Married couples our age don't have sex

* I want to try spicing things up but he/she has said no in the past

* I don't feel good about my body anymore

* Low libido or lack of sex drive due to physical or emotional issues

* Stress, fear and anxiety about life in general

* Conflicts within the relationship outside of the bedroom

* Medications that decrease libido and performance

Many of the issues mentioned are perfectly normal and a part of a long term relationship. People do become familiar with each other, fall into a comfortable pattern of intimate relationships or even slowly move away from sexual intimacy.

Sex Has Benefits

Research has shown that married couples with an active sex life tend to live longer, have stronger emotional connections to each other, have a lower divorce rate and remain healthier even as they age. So, despite what may seem a natural downward progression to a relationship, there is sound evidence that keeping a healthy, active and satisfying sexual relationship with your husband is really a benefit throughout your life.

It is important for married couples to realize that every individual is different and rarely are two people completely matched with regards to their sex drive. Learning to read your husband's signals, as well as giving out the right signals yourself, is a true skill, and one that can help form a much better relationship.

Taking care of your physical as well as your emotional self is a major factor in being active and involved in an intimate relationship. Some of the work needs to start with you before you can expect to see a change in your husband's responsiveness. However, if you both begin to consciously change your attitudes towards your intimate relationship you will be amazed at how you can discover each other all over again.

One key issue for couples to keep in mind, as they work to improve their sex life, is that they shouldn't be trying to compare themselves to statistics and information that they may find on the internet or in books. Everyone is different and there is no reason that you have to match the national average for number of times you have sex. Interestingly enough, in a recent Woman's Day report in February of 2012 people reported that the average number of times they had sex per year was one hundred and three, which is roughly twice a week.

Furthermore, researchers have found that the more often people have sex the more likely they are to want more sex. Withholding sex from your husband, either wilfully or because of physical or emotional issues, will result in a decrease in the likelihood of sex. Increasing your attention to your husband and sending a clear message that you are in the mood will simply enhance the chance of more frequent intimate moments.

This book will provide simple, effective and, yes, even practical ways to jump-start your sex life again. You can start out slowly and stay within your comfort zone at first, but remember that the more you try the more likely you are to create that wonderful experience for you both.

Let's Get 2 Physical

All intimate couple relationships have some sort of physical aspect; and this is the area where most couples report having difficulty as their relationship continues over time. There are many factors that influence the physical aspect of a relationship. While not all physical issues could or should be modified, there are lots of ways to enhance your own personal physical confidence as well as that of your husband.

This chapter will look at some of the significant ways in which men and women can work towards creating a better physical relationship. Not surprisingly, many of these techniques and ideas focus on health and healthy living, but also on emotional and mental health issues.

One Sexy Wife- With Confidence

● ●

When a woman doesn't feel good about herself it is hard for her to enjoy a physical relationship. Often self-confidence, also known as self-esteem or self-worth, is a very complex emotional component in an individual's life. Women who have a high level of self-confidence are more inclined to:

* Try new things

* Speak their mind openly about their desires

* Respond to their husband's needs and desires

* Get into a romantic mood

* Be spontaneous

* Focus on the other person

* Enjoy sex

* Have a healthy and positive view of their own body and their husband's body

* Learn about enhancing sexual experiences

* Engage in foreplay

In addition, both men and women with good levels of self-confidence are more likely to use physical touch and eye contact with each other throughout the day, to send those signals that the evening is sure to be special.

Self-confidence and self-esteem aren't something that you can just snap your fingers and add to your repertoire, but you can start by avoiding comparisons of your body and physical attributes with those of others. Often the biggest cause of loss of self-confidence, particularly with women, is comparing themselves to models, actresses and other women.

While most people understand in their hearts that looking like a twenty-something model is unrealistic, somehow the message isn't getting to the brain. Instead, listen to your husband and respond to his positive comments about your looks and your body, and just stop comparing yourself to anyone else.

Couples that find each other attractive both mentally as well as physically are much more likely to engage in frequent sex, so having a positive sense of who you are will really help.

Food, Fuel, and Exercise

Staying in good shape is always going to boost both your self-confidence mentally and your willingness to have physical contact with your husband. In some relationships lack of physical contact is really noticeable if one spouse feels "fat," "unattractive" or "undesirable" because of his or her weight.

Dieting isn't recommended, especially the crash diets that promise huge weight loss amounts in very short periods of time. Rather, consider a lifestyle change that involves becoming more active as a couple and also making healthier food choices.

By working on improving your healthy lifestyle you will not only see changes in your physical body but you may also discover new ways to build in together-time. Couples that do more activities together tend to have stronger emotional and physical relationships, so it actually will address more than one aspect of your intimate life at the same time.

Diets that consist of a balance of fresh fruits, vegetables, lean meats and proteins, and whole grains can also help the body function more effectively. Minimizing refined sugars and carbohydrates as well as limiting the intake of stimulants such as caffeine will also help with keeping your body in balance. W

hile a glass of wine or a social drink isn't going to be a problem, overconsumption of alcohol will cause a decrease in your overall sex drive and will also impact other aspects of your marriage as well.

Keep in mind that developing a healthy lifestyle and increasing your activity level doesn't mean that you have to go into training or just jog every day.

There are many great fun and relationship-building activities that couples can do together to get in shape and build those emotional bonds.

Suggestions for fun, moderate to high exercise level activities you can do together include:

* Going for a romantic walk at the beach, lake, park or even around your neighborhood

* Kayaking or white-water rafting

* Going swimming

* Roller skating or ice skating to your favorite music

* Taking out a gym membership together

* Waterskiing or snow skiing getaways

* Gardening and working together on the yard

* Walking, jogging or running in a charity event as a team

* Camping and hiking together through the mountains

* Cycling

* Horseback riding

* Ballroom dancing

* Playing your favorite sports on a co-ed team

Exercising together in playful yet active events or settings is a great way to bond emotionally, while gaining a better body and a healthier lifestyle. Don't forget that being in better physical shape translates into benefits in the bedroom. Research has shown that exercise has a positive impact on:

1. Stress reduction: Less stress means more time to focus on your husband and enjoying the time you are together. Stress also decreases sex drive, so eliminating stress from your life is essential to building a better physical and emotionally healthy marriage.

2. Endurance: When you exercise on a routine basis your muscles build up greater endurance to physical movement and activity. This means that you will be able to stay in one position for a longer period of time, or even be more adventurous in the positions you try out for the first time.

3. Cardio: When your heart is strong and actively pumping blood you have more energy and are less easily fatigued. This will also increase your blood flow to all the parts of your body, including the sex organs, enhancing the physical experience.

4. Strength: Like muscular endurance, being strong enough to support your body in a variety of positions is one of the best ways to feel confident and comfortable in trying out new positions.

5. Hormones: Women who work out routinely tend to produce more of the endorphins or pleasure hormones, which contribute to the enjoyment of sex and also to getting into the mood.

Interestingly enough, sex itself is a good form of exercise. It is estimated that fairly vigorous sexual activity will burn approximately two hundred calories per thirty minutes. While this isn't the same as a half hour on the treadmill, it will continue to improve your cardio, strength, endurance and calorie burning capacity.

Pampering Yourself

Part of the physical aspect of sex is to feel good about yourself. While most people continually work on their weight and body shape, it helps to pamper yourself physically to really enjoy sex.

Pampering yourself starts with making you feel sexy. For women this can include taking a long, luxurious, scented bath. This can include candles, a glass of wine and perhaps some romantic music. You may also want to consider a pedicure and manicure, a trip to the spa once or twice a month and perhaps a facial on a routine basis.

You can also try different fragrances that can have very interesting effects on both your own mood as well as that of your husband. Since the sense of smell is one of the most primitive senses, it can evoke strong mental images, moods and desires. Finding a fragrance that stimulates your husband can really help create the mood and allow you to also feel sexy.

Taking care of your body is a way to show your husband how much you care about him. Try some additional little tricks such as smoothing your elbows, knees, hands and feet, to provide additional softness during intimacy and foreplay.

There are many products on the market today that help all skin types feel smooth and luxurious, with or without adding a fragrance. If you are wearing a favorite perfume opt for a unscented skin cream or lotion, to avoid having too many different scents at one time.

You may also want to consider having a couple's day at the spa as a joint pampering treat. Engage in some soothing massages and facials, or even a relaxing time in a sauna or one of the heated baths at the spa. You don't need to do everything together; do something just for yourself and plan to make it a day of indulgence, with the anticipation of a wonderful evening together when your spa day is done.

Great Energy Levels Lead To Great Sex

As mentioned in the exercise information, having a high energy level means longer, more satisfying sexual interactions. However, high energy levels don't mean having sex in a rush, but they do allow you to enjoy vigorous, extended sexual intimacy that is the key to satisfaction for both of you.

One of the best ways to ensure that you have, and maintain, high energy levels is to get enough rest: approximately eight solid hours of sleep every day of the week. If you have kids, are a light sleeper or have health issues that make sleeping for eight hours difficult, you may simply cause lower energy levels, leading to decreased libido and enjoyment of sex.

Try to change your schedule and talk to your doctor about how you can safely and naturally get the recommended sleep level per day. In some cases herbal teas, yoga, relaxation techniques or just adding a bit more exercise to your day can really help out in getting better sleep.

To improve the quality of your sleep, avoid the following for at least four hours prior to bedtime:

* Caffeinated drinks such as coffee, tea and most types of soda

* Tobacco

* Chocolate – in large amounts

* Sugary drinks, including fruit juices from concentrate

* Eating heavy meals

* Medications with stimulant ingredients

* Heavy exercise

* Avoid watching television or playing (or working) on the computer for at least an hour before bedtime.

Try the following to get a good night's sleep, so you wake up relaxed, refreshed and energized:

* Drink warm milk or herbal teas

* Take a warm bath

* Listen to soft, relaxing music

* Read a good book

* Eat some fresh fruit or protein at least three hours before bedtime

For some couples, sleeping in the same bed is not always conducive to getting a good night's sleep. Snoring, a spouse who wakes up often or moves constantly in the bed, or talks in his or her sleep can often prevent the other spouse from getting the relaxing night he or she needs. Not only does this lead to tension, stress and even anger, but it will decrease energy levels and reduce the chance for intimacy.

Talk about how your sexual relationship can grow and prosper under these difficult circumstances.

Enhancing Sexual Experiences

There are a number of medical and psychological factors that can decrease sexual drive, performance and enjoyment. For many couples this is a never-discussed topic but one that certainly should be addressed within the marriage.

It is estimated that approximately 35% of men between the ages of 40 and 70 have moderate to severe problems with impotency, also known as erectile dysfunction or ED. An additional 15% have mild forms of ED that cause feelings of inadequacy in their sexual relationships. Men also can have a decrease in their libido or sex drive, but this is less common, with approximately 15 to 16% of the entire male population estimated to have a loss of interest in sex.

Women, on the other hand, tend to have more problems with low sex drive or loss of libido. It is estimated that approximately 30 to 40% of all females past puberty will, at some time in their lives, have little or no interest in sex. Often this is hormonal in nature and may coincide with pregnancy, lactation, perimenopause or menopause.

For both men and women, stress from work, financial problems, relationships or family can all lead to a period of time where sex just does not seem as important, desirable or worth the effort. However, research shows that couples that work together to redevelop their sexual relationship and intimacy are more likely to stay together, report being happier, and also work through the problems that are causing the lack of desire for intimacy.

Prescription Medications That Affect Libido

Men are actually more fortunate than women when it comes to being able to take a pill to help with erectile dysfunction or other sex related problems. Unless there is a health concern with sex, or a possible conflict with other medications, men tend to tolerate ED medications very well. Of course, there are possible side-effects to these medications and it is very important for both partners to understand the signs of an adverse reaction to the medications.

Common mediations that are prescribed to help with ED include:

* Viagra   * Cialis   * Levitra

All of these medications work to increase the blood flow to the penis, allowing for a full, lasting erection. While the medications are different, they work very much the same, typically with good results. There are variances in how long the medication is effective, as well as how quickly the results from taking the medication will be noticed.

Women with low sex drive or loss of libido will soon be able to take their own versions of Viagra. While there are currently no specific prescription medications on the market to deal with the physical side of women's sexual experiences, many doctors find that low dosage antidepressant medications may have a positive impact on female libido.

Natural Options to Increase Libido

There is a wide range of herbal, holistic and naturopathic remedies marketed over the internet, in health food stores and even in drug stores. Most of these so called "natural stimulants" or "natural sex enhancers" are not tested in a controlled setting, so their effectiveness is typically a claim made by the company trying to sell the product.

With that being disclosed, there are some treatments that have long been used in many cultures around the world. It is essential to talk to your physician before using any herbal supplement as they can have severely adverse side-effects or interactions with current medications. It is also important to check if there isn't an underlying medical condition that is impacting your sexual pleasure and enjoyment before starting on any of these treatments.

Some options for natural sex-enhancing treatments include:

   * Acupuncture – for both men and women

   * Arginine – used to increase blood flow and circulation

   * Ginseng – more commonly associated with male performance

   * Pomegranate juice – high in antioxidants

   * Ginkgo biloba – may be suitable for men and women who have low sex drive or libido without sexual functioning problems

* Zinc supplements – may increase testosterone in both men and women

* Vitamin E – essential precursor to the development of the sex hormones in both men and women

* Don quai – a traditional treatment for all types of female reproductive disorders

* Yohimbine and Yohimbe – perhaps the oldest treatment for ED, it is potentially dangerous for men who are sensitive to the alkaloid found in the herbal preparation

It is very important to know exactly what is in the supplement before considering ingesting the pill, capsule or even drinking a tea made with the herbs.

Some of these herbal combinations are very powerful stimulants that may be fatal to individuals with heart conditions, high blood pressure or other metabolic disorders. Avoid any type of herbal supplements until consulting with your doctor.

Sexy Foods

There are some foods that are just romantic and associated with intimacy and desire. Chocolate-covered strawberries are probably the first food that comes to mind, but there are foods all over the world that are believed to enhance desire and to stimulate sexual activity for both men and women.

These so-called aphrodisiac foods are found all over the world, some of which are fairly common.

Whether or not these foods can actually increase sexual desire and get you in the mood is not really the issue. A lot of sexual excitement and anticipation is in the mind; so if eating some of these foods gets you in the mood, why not give them a try?

Foods from different cultures that are believed to enhance sexual desire include:

Celery	Lettuce	Arugula
Saffron	Dark Chocolate	Artichokes
Oysters	Truffles	Bananas
Vanilla	Avocado	Figs
Honey	Ginger	Pineapple
Strawberries	Raspberries	

In many countries red wine is also considered to be an aphrodisiac, especially when combined with dark chocolate.

It's Emotional

Both married men and women report that sex is much more satisfying when there is an emotional connection with their spouse. It is true that this component of sexual intimacy is more important to women than men, but men also want to have a strong emotional bond with their wives if they are in the marriage for the duration.

Forming this emotional connection with the other person takes effort, planning and commitment to each other, but the payoff is a very strong union that translates into a strong desire for each other, both physically and intimately.

In addition to increasing and sustaining desire, having a strong emotional attachment allows more personal freedom within the marriage. Couples are more likely to try new sexual ideas, work harder to please their spouses and strive to keep the physical part of the marriage front and center.

Most couples, especially those who have been married for a significant amount of time, start to forget about all the wonderful things that each spouse brings to the experience of being together.

You may find that you fall into bed at night exhausted from a day at the office or looking after the kids, and fail to notice that "come-hither" look in your spouse's eye. Or perhaps even worse, you notice it, but pretend not to since you are tired or really not in the mood yourself.

Over time this gradually leads to both a physical and emotional distance between you. This doesn't mean you can't say no every now and then, but it does mean that you need to find ways to connect emotionally so you will look forward to connecting sexually.

It is never too late to start noticing your spouse anew -- recreating that emotional thrill and excitement you both had when you were together at the beginning of your marriage.

The Strong Connection

Emotional connections require work and a conscious effort to reach out to your spouse on more than just a physical level. Keeping the emotional connection strong and alive in your marriage isn't difficult, especially if you develop healthy habits with regards to giving and receiving emotional support and encouragement from your spouse.

Some of the easiest ways to stay connected are to look for ways to highlight and compliment each other throughout the day. A good way to get this started is to make one meaningful compliment, notice one positive thing the other person does, or say thank you to the person for something he or she did each and every day. These words of connection and emotional support and encouragement need to be from the heart, not just hollow compliments to stroke the ego.

A good communication tool for building a strong emotional connection is to describe the specific behavior that lets him know how it benefited you and how much you appreciate his effort. This is much better than just a "thanks for your help today" type of statement. It shows not only that you were paying attention but also that you thought enough of the gesture to voice your thanks.

Saying that you love him is also an important part of keeping your connection strong. For some couples saying "I love you" is routine, usually when everyone leaves the house for work and when everyone goes to bed at night. Instead of just staying in the routine add an "I love you" throughout the day. Some suggestions to add an "I love you" statement:

* A note in the briefcase, computer case, or lunch box

* An "I love you" text message at a random time when your husband is away from you

* When he gets home from work (or you both return)

* Calling him at work or when he is away on business, just to say how much you love him

* Emails

* Sending a card by traditional mail to his place of work, just because you care

Keep in mind that for some individuals really public displays of "I love you" messages may be more of a turn-off than a turn-on. Always gauge or watch your husband's reaction to your communication and make adjustments to stay within his comfort zone.

However, text messages and emails shouldn't be a problem for most people; you may find he secretly looks forward to the signal that there is a message or email. (Be mindful of office protocol or security regulations that govern the workplace.)

Plan Ahead
• • • • • • •

If you don't have an active love life, or if it isn't as active as you would like it to be, you may want to start planning ahead about how to motivate your husband.

Spontaneity is great, but you may have to really plan for the best time to have sex for those individuals who work long hours, have to deal with very challenging jobs at home or at work, or who have a lower sex drive.

You may also have to rethink the best time for sex. Waiting until after the kids are in bed, dishes are done and the work is done for the day may leave you both at your lowest emotional and physical energy levels.

If this is the case you may want to set the alarm clock a bit earlier in the morning, allowing you to spend time with each other when you are rested, relaxed and rejuvenated from a good night's sleep.

You may also want to plan for some adult alone-time when you get home from work or on those lazy weekends when lounging around in bed and reconnecting with each other is much more possible and less rushed.

Planning ahead for sex is also a great way to get you in the mood. You can find a bit of extra time to pamper yourself that day, preparing for a special evening to enjoy time with your husband.

Remember that a lot of desire and sexual drive is developed through anticipation and expectation, so don't keep your plans a secret. Share you desire for your husband and express your plans for the afternoon, evening, morning or whenever you want to be intimate. This will only help him get in the mood mentally, ensuring enhanced arousal when it is time to be together.

If you have children or other adults living in your home, they can inhibit your ability to relax and enjoy each other sexually. It can be helpful to arrange getting them out of the house, at least sometimes, by engaging overnight care, babysitters, or by asking friends to have the kids stay with them, as a way to surprise your husband.

This can allow you to really go back to the beginning of your relationship, before parenthood, when you didn't have to be careful of making too much noise or keeping the bedroom door closed.

While it may sound almost oversimplified, these small little details all send a very specific message to your husband. They say that you care, you have been waiting for this moment, and you want everything to be perfect for you both.

The effort that you make in planning ahead for intimate moments doesn't have to happen every time you make love, but it certainly will be appreciated when it does occur. Planning ahead also has a lot to do with setting the atmosphere.

Sending Sex Signals

While it may sound cliché, most spouses can recognize the "come-hither" look in each other's eyes. Sending signals early and often that you want to have a romantic interlude is a great way to build anticipation and arousal before the physical contact occurs.

Setting the emotional tone for intimacy can start hours, or even a day or two, before sex actually occurs. Sending signals is perhaps one of the oldest and most instinctual things that humans do, but you can also make them very intentional, yet still subtle; perfect for creating both a bit of mystery and anticipation.

Some signals that will definitely get the message across of your desire for a sexual encounter include:

 * Pampering your husband with a favorite meal or food item

* Suggesting a meeting at a favorite lounge or restaurant that has a romantic atmosphere

* A long, romantic kiss before going off to work or when getting home

* Dressing provocatively

* A visit to his work or office, just to say that you can't wait for him to get home

* Extra attention to your physical appearance

* Wearing his favorite outfit or color

* Using messages of love during the day

* Holding hands and touching

* Sharing a shower

* Talking about your desire and your plans

* Long, sexual glances

Giving off as many signals as possible about your plans for intimacy is important. This both cues your husband and helps you to stay intense in your desire.

Building Anticipation
Date Your Husband

For many marriages, juggling kids, home, careers and a social life, makes it difficult to find time to spend just with each other in the kinds of romantic activities you could when you were first married. Everything seems to have turned into an endless cycle of work, family, kids and sleep.

However, there is a way to bring that anticipation and desire back into your life without having to run away from the kids.

Dating your husband is a great way to set aside planned time with each other. Dates should have some ground rules to ensure they are successful and don't end up being sabotaged by kids, family members or your work.

Set The Date

● ● ● ● ● ● ● ●

Many people don't see scheduling time together as very romantic. Rather, they see it as planned, forced or even manipulated. It can also seem to be selfish and perhaps even unfair to kids and other members of the family. For the sake of your relationship as a couple, though, it really is an effective way to keep the romance alive in your relationship.

Scheduling dates was normal before you where married, so why shouldn't it be when you are in the same home? After all, you don't just show up at a date's home; you call ahead to set a date and time, so everyone can prepare and anticipate the evening, day or afternoon together.

Married couples that routinely use date nights wouldn't go back to just trying to squeeze in some romance. Different couples like different options, so it is really up to you both to decide what works best.

One popular option is to have one night every week as date night. Often this is a Friday or Saturday evening, but any evening or day is perfect, depending on work schedules.

It is important to get out of the house, and spend some quality time together, such as going out to eat, dancing, enjoying a drink together or going to a movie, concert, theater or other type of event.

Some couples prefer to spend time together outdoors. They may choose to go for a hike, picnic, fishing or bird watching. It really doesn't matter what you do; what matters is that you enjoy doing it, spend time connecting and get a chance to be alone together.

Other couples prefer to have a more variable schedule. They may take turns to decide where to go on the date, who contacts whom to set up the date and on what day of the week it is. This option typically works best for couples with fairly predictable work schedules, and that don't have problems in trying to coordinate evenings or days off with each other.

There need to be some ground rules: During the date the focus is not be on finances, problems with the kids, issues at work or any other stressful conversations. This is a chance for the two of you to enjoy each other's company and remember why you love each other so much. It all goes back to keeping a strong emotional aspect to your relationship.

In addition to just not talking about kids, the house or work, you also need to talk to the children and let them know that this is your time alone together. Plan some special events with the entire family as well, and your children will understand that date night is for the parents, and that there will be lots of activities for the whole family at other times. Find a babysitter or family member the kids like spending time with and whom you trust; then turn the cell phones on vibrate and just go and enjoy.

Only respond to emergency calls. Always have an alternate emergency contact option for the caregiver, making sure they understand that it is for emergency purposes only.

Flirt
● ● ●

Some people are just natural flirts, while others have to work at learning the skills needed to be a successful flirt. With all the different instant communications available to couples today, flirting both high and low tech, with relative privacy, is easier than ever.

Flirting by sending signals is a really low tech version of the skill, such as loving, desire-filled glances, blowing kisses, and dressing in a desirable and sexy way. Remember that flirting can include conversation, brief physical contact of an intimate nature, or body language.

There are many ways in which women, in particular, can send suggestive messages just by their body posture and position. For example, touching the hair, face and throat is seen as a flirting gesture, as it draws the eye towards the location of contact. Giggling and smiling can also be very flirtatious; and men are often very clear in sending messages with both their smiles and their tone of voice.

New technology has opened up the door for a whole new type of flirting. Texting, chat messages and emails can send a clear message, but it is important to think about where these messages may be viewed and how uncomfortable the message could be if viewed in the wrong arena.

Sending messages that contain obvious or overtly sexual connotation in a workplace environment could be a disaster, so always be aware of where your husband may be when he gets your message.

It is a good idea to read through your message before you hit the "send" button, to make sure it isn't too sexual in nature and might be problematic if someone else were to see it. You may want to reconsider how to word the message so your husband understands the message, but anyone else wouldn't see the flirting component.

Setting the Stage for Romance

The atmosphere or the environment can be important in sending a message to your spouse that you are in the mood. For some couples a house full of kid's toys, barking dogs or piles of work to do is simply a mood killer. While you may not be able to totally remove all these obstacles to a romantic interlude you certainly can minimize their impact.

Setting a romantic tone for the evening, afternoon or whenever you find time to enjoy each other's company doesn't have to be elaborate or stressful. Look for ways to make your home more relaxing, seductive and private -- a sure way to provide just the atmosphere you need.

Tips and Ideas for Romance

Most people have some tried and true simple ways to make the bedroom look a bit less like just a room to sleep in, and more like a romantic spot in the home. Some of the added touches can be left all the time to help make your bedroom a true sanctuary, where you both enjoy spending time with each other.

First and foremost, get rid of all the technology stuff that isn't romantic at all. The laptop, desktop computer, television, telephone, cell phone or anything else that connects you to the outside world should be temporarily banished.

Not only does this prevent interruptions but it also sets a much more relaxing and much less distracting environment for romance. After all, you want to be focused on each other and your experience together, not on the television or what is on the computer.

You will also want to remove the items in the room that remind you of work that has to be done. The laundry basket needs to be put in the closet or in the laundry room; stacks of paperwork should be put in the office or at least out of sight in a drawer or filing cabinet. This prevents you from letting your mind drift to all the pressures of the outside world that are just waiting for you.

This help with your ability to stay "in the moment" with your husband, but you are also more likely to avoid jumping up out of bed to head back to work immediately after making love.

In addition to removing all those work and daily grind items from your bedroom, there are some other things that you can add to enhance the enjoyment of the atmosphere. You can try one or all of these things, or even save a few for those very special occasions.

Aromatherapy and Scents

One of the strongest senses that humans possess is the sense of smell. How many times do you immediately remember a person, a moment or an intense memory when you smell a waft of perfume or cologne, even on a complete stranger? Tapping into the power of your sense of smell can trigger powerful emotional and hormonal responses in both you and your husband, and help to signal that you have a desire to be intimate.

Essential oils used in aromatherapy are a great way to add a subtle scent to the room without being overpowering. Just a small drop or two of the oil on a diffuser or oil warmer can add a luscious and romantic touch to your next encounter. Some essential oils can also be used in massage oils. Not all oils should be applied to the skin, however, so be sure to research this or talk to an aromatherapist before getting started. Some of the best essential oils recommended to increase the mood and stimulate sex drives include:

• **Ylang Ylang:** Used in the East, this wonderfully sweeter-smelling oil is popular with both men and women. It needs to be used in very small amounts (one or two drops only), as it can be overpowering for some. Try starting with one drop and increase it if you both find the scent pleasurable.

• **Jasmine:** Again, a sweeter, flowery smell, Jasmine is often considered a powerful night flower. While it can be used on its own as an air scent, you can also add a drop or two to a warm bath or combine it with sandalwood or a citrus-based oil for a wonderfully exotic and completely unique combination.

• **Rose otto:** This flowery smelling essential oil is great for massage oils, especially for women. It is thought to enhance a woman's libido and strengthen sexual desire.

• **Lavender:** Long known for its relaxing qualities, lavender can aid in soothing people who are stressed or anxious, so they can enjoy each other and their time together. Don't use more than a drop or two at a time.

• **Cinnamon:** Men in particular respond to the smell of the less floral types of oils. Cinnamon is considered a scent of passion and spice, and there is some scientific evidence that it stimulates blood flow. Other food type scents with aphrodisiac qualities include vanilla, nutmeg and chocolate.

• *Cedarwood:* Another very manly scent, cedarwood is an earthy, sexual scent that both men and women respond well to. You may also want to try sandalwood, which has a more distinctive scent.

• *Patchouli:* Very popular with those who enjoy musky, yet slightly sweet fragrances. Patchouli is helpful in relieving tension while also stimulating sex drive.

You may also choose to simply go with a favorite perfume; just be sure not to use too much. In addition, avoid mixing multiple scents as the result can be horrific, to say the least.

If you are using fragrances on your body dab a bit on your neck, your wrists and your erogenous zones. For most women that will be around the breasts, behind the knees and the inner thighs. Again, just a slight amount is all you need as you and your partner's senses will already be heightened.

Lighting
● ● ● ● ●

Romantic lighting is important and should provide a comfortable level of light to allow you to see each other. Lovemaking in the dark is never as satisfying for a couple that wants an emotional connection. Eye contact during foreplay and sex can be intensely arousing, so don't keep you or your partner in the dark.

Candles have long been a romantic favorite. You can have one or two larger candles or a collection of smaller candles. Of course, there is one concern with candles: for safety reasons, they need to be extinguished prior to your going to sleep.

For some couples a better option is a very soft lighting source, such as a bedside lamp with a darker shade and a dimmer switch. This can allow you to have soft light that can easily be turned off when you are ready to sleep. Colors of shades that can help set a romantic mood include greens, reds and blues; choose one that complements you bedding and your favorite colors.

Lights that give off a soft glow or a natural light are very soothing and romantic, and allow a gentle and almost misty style of lighting. These are often wall-mount lights that highlight the area around the bed without making you feel like you are in the spotlight.

These lights are available in very romantic styles and can even be artificial candle-style fixtures that mimic a real flame or old style gas light.

Your Boudoire

● ● ● ● ● ● ● ● ●

An easy way to add a change to your bedroom is to simply change your bedding. You could go for a satin sheet set in your favorite color or a beautiful soft Egyptian cotton sheet set that just makes you feel sexy the moment you get into bed.

Having a few different sets of sheets really does have an impact on your love life. When your husband sees the satin sheets on the bed he is already aware of what you have planned for what's to come. This helps to build anticipation and enhances those other signals you have been sending. And even he can change the sheets to indicate his mood!

Although going to a hotel, bed and breakfast or a cabin can be a romantic change of pace, it isn't always financially practical or reasonable. By switching up your bed and making your room look just a bit different you can get that "romantic getaway" feeling right in your own home.

Tunes that Tantalize

● ● ● ● ● ● ● ● ● ● ●

Some couples differ about what kinds of music are romantic. If you don't already have a list of romantic songs you may want to make it a discussion point for your next evening away from the kids, or your next car ride together. Creating a list of songs of your favorite romantic singers can be a great couple's activity to add to the romance of the bedroom.

The Setting

While the conversation so far has focused on creating the bedroom as the place of romance in the house, there is no reason why you can't romance each other in other rooms of the house.

A lovely evening spent enjoying each other's company by the fireplace or with a glass of wine in the den can make for a relaxing and romantic time. Restricting your lovemaking to the bedroom may, in part, creates boredom and an expectation of routine rather than enjoyment in being together.

Just keep in mind that any room in the home can be the spot for some spontaneous romance, so don't get hung up on just the bedroom.

Foreplay

Sending early and clear messages about your desire, as well as building anticipation of your time together, are two sure ways to improve your sex life. Another very important aspect of lovemaking for both men and women, but more particularly for women, is foreplay.

Foreplay can include flirting, as discussed earlier, but it also needs to include some very intentional physical contact. This romantic touch doesn't need to be overtly sexual in nature, and for many men and women it really doesn't need to be even subtly sexual.

Physical contact is a deeply human need for both physical and mental health. Sex is the most intimate physical contact, and can be the most satisfying. To improve your sex life, start adding a bit more casual touching in your relationship; you will be amazed at the results.

Very socially appropriate types of touching between married couples include:

1. **Holding hands:** This is a very traditional way for couples to remain in close physical contact with each other. Try adding a subtle stroking motion with your thumb or fingers on your husband's hand and see the response that you get.

2. **Hands on the arm or leg:** A gentle and brief touch on the knee, upper leg or the forearm can be a very romantic gesture. You should also maintain eye contact as much as possible when making this gesture; this combines both an emotional message and the physical contact.

3. **Arms around the waist or shoulders:** Similar to holding hands, married couples often link arms around their waists or their shoulders to bring their bodies closer together. Try adding a gentle rub on the arm or a slow movement of the hand down the waist or hips to add to the sensuality of the touch.

4. **Kissing:** Kissing, without becoming too extreme, is a socially acceptable way to show your love and desire for your spouse. Just don't get too car-

ried away, especially in work environments, as it may actually cause your spouse to be uncomfortable or even resentful of the attention. Talking about what is OK and what isn't, and what both of your comfort levels are with regards to kissing, is an important conversation to have.

5. **Stroking the face or neck:** Reaching over to run a gentle hand down your husband's cheek or neck is a very sexy move that is also subtle and very appropriate. Again, eye contact will enhance the mood and clearly send an "I want you" signal.

Foreplay in private can be much more sexual and intimate in nature. Full body contact in hugging or kissing, and when being attentive to each other, is a great way to signal your desire. Of course, foreplay can also include undressing each other slowly and sensually, as well as giving each other massages, or simply exploring each other's bodies.

Foreplay needs to start early and can extend for long periods of time before you actually do make love. Many couples admit that sex becomes a routine and an expectation, almost as if it is a timed event rather than an enjoyment of each other. By extending the foreplay outside of the act of intercourse you will sustain your sexual arousal and enjoyment, leading to a more satisfying sexual encounter.

Set the Mood with Massage

• • • • • • • • • • • • • • • • • • •

Massages shared between married couples, or going to a spa, or having a massage therapist come into the home are all great ideas. Of course, if you give each other massages you can incorporate a lot more foreplay and sensual components, which can be a nice added touch.

Massages don't have to be professional quality; rather they simply need to stimulate the other person and signal your desire for intimacy. Massaging the feet, back, legs and arms is a great way to make a lot of physical contact and bring pleasure to your spouse.

Massages do increase blood stimulation to the muscles being massaged and they are great when combined with a romantic atmosphere to reduce tension and stress, to put you both in the mood.

Try adding massage oils to your massage to change things up a bit. These massage oils may be scented and infused with the essential oils called "couple's oils" that heat or cool when applied to the skin.

There are also oils on the market that give a tingling sensation to the skin; very sexual and very pleasant for most people to experience. Always test a small area on yourself or your husband before using the oils on a large part of the skin to check for allergic reactions. In addition, avoid using these oils on the genital areas unless specifically indicated as safe on the product label.

If you aren't sure how to give a massage, or if you have never had a massage yourself, you really do need to do some fun research. Book yourself into a spa or have a massage therapist come to the house and experience firsthand just how good it can make you feel.

The internet has a lot of great videos and do-it-yourself tutorials on how to give different types of massages. Just go for the basics; after all, this is only a part of the foreplay activities, not the plan for the entire night!

Overnight Romantic Get-Aways

If you can afford time away from the house, kids and your busy schedules, try a romantic getaway, even if just for an evening. Plan a dinner at a favorite restaurant, a night at a movie, dancing or just walking along a sunset beach, and then plan a night away at a local hotel. You don't have to go far; just a change from the house is all it takes to jump-start your sex life.

Many people who travel for business have points or rewards programs that entitle them to free nights at hotels. Plan to use these free nights with your spouse, and plan them at different times, perhaps between stressful holidays or after dealing with back-to-school preps for the kids.

Lots of hotels, even very high-end luxury hotels, offer discount rates if you book a night during the week. Monday through Thursday typically will be your best bet for a low-cost night at a very extravagant and luxury hotel.

While you don't have to ask for the honeymoon suite, this could be a wonderful additional romantic touch every now and then. Again, midweek rates and off-season rates can be incredibly affordable, often with breakfast or additional perks thrown in as part of the honeymoon suite price.

You Are the Stage- Sexy Lingerie

There is a wide variety in evening wear. Adding a bit of lingerie to your wardrobe collection helps to get you in the mood, and makes you feel sexy. Your husband is sure to appreciate the effort.

Finding sexy lingerie that also makes you feel comfortable and confident is sometimes a bit daunting. The internet has certainly made this much easier for women, since you can buy online and don't have to spend time browsing through lingerie or costume stores. Keep in mind that some lingerie can be found in costume outlets for a fraction of the price.

Lingerie can include those revealing little wisps of lace and satiny fabric, but it can also be lovely nightgowns, teddies and even very traditional kinds of costume outfits. The sexy French maid, the naughty nurse or the Playboy bunny can all be a great way to surprise your husband with a night that promises to be anything but boring.

If you haven't considered adding lingerie to your evenings together try starting with something basic. Then you can decide if you enjoy the experience and add more elaborate styles of lingerie and costumes.

There are specialty shops that feature leather, vinyl, fabric or custom-designed costumes and lingerie that are perfect for fantasy evenings. Since you can order online you really can shop the world in the privacy of your own home, and find the specific lingerie that will help enhance your desire and attraction for each other.

Learn Each 7 Other Well

If you have been in your marriage for a while you probably think that you already know all about your spouse. This assumption is what is most problematic in most relationships. You believe you know what they want, need and enjoy, so you never bother to ask.

One of the biggest factors in improving your love life and your sexual interactions with each other is to actually get to know each other all over again. Forget what you think he likes in bed; start exploring as if you were entering into the relationship for the first time.

This may seem a little odd at first, but you will soon find out what you want from the relationship with regards to sex, as well as what your husband's desires really are.

Fantasy Options and Sexual Wants

● ● ● ● ● ● ● ● ● ● ● ● ● ● ● ● ● ●

Talking with your spouse about what he enjoys in sex and what he has always been curious about, but hasn't tried yet, is an important first step.

It may be difficult to get the conversation started but with a few tips you will be able to get a clearer picture of what each of you wants, as well as any fantasy sexual desires you both may have.

The following are tips for conversation starters with your husband about sex:

* Talk about why the conversation is occurring – explaining that you want to make your sex life together better gives a clear meaning to the conversation.

* Talk about your fantasy sex life, and ask your husband about his.

* Never be judgmental in a negative way or he won't share his ideas and true needs, wants and desires.

* Don't be afraid to ask for more information in a loving and supportive way.

* Listen, so he gives information to you, and vice versa.

* Start with just one thing; you don't have to discuss everything all at once. As you both build up a comfort level with this type of discussion you can become more detailed and specific in the information you share.

* Don't have the discussion in the middle of sex. Have this conversation when you both are relaxed and in a positive mental state.

* Keep the information private. Don't share your husband's fantasies with your friends; this is a real trust breaker.

* Incorporate what he wants and what you want into each sexual encounter as it makes sense. You don't have to make every sexual encounter into a fantasy night, but you now know how to add that extra spark when the time and mood is right.

* Don't shut your husband down when he wants to talk, especially if this is something he hasn't done before. This can be a bit awkward for you both at first, but with practice, and an improvement in your sex life, it will become a part of your intimate relationship that will just keep building.

Pillow Talk

● ● ● ● ● ● ●

Talking before, during and after sex is a part of being connected as a couple. However, not everyone wants talk during sex and not everyone enjoys pillow-talk afterwards.

If you are a talker, or if your husband enjoys communicating during sex, you may be able to make that part of improving your love life together. You can instruct him how to provide the right amount of pleasure, and talking sexy yourself can help to set the mood.

Of course, reading your spouse to see if he is into this type of talking during or after sex is important.

When providing instruction during sex it is important not to come across as bossy, demanding or with an "it's all about my pleasure" attitude. Many spouses are very good at helping the other person know what to do in a gentle, loving way. In return, they are also willing to follow the other person's instructions. For others it may take practice.

The taboo about talking or telling the other person what to do to make you feel good is a real problem in many marriages. After all, how would the other person know what makes you feel sexy so that you reach sexual satisfaction if you cannot communicate the information?

If you don't do this at least occasionally (and it doesn't need to happen every time you make love), you should talk to your spouse about it. You can always make it into a first sex fantasy, playing as if you didn't know anything about him and requiring his verbal commands.

Reciprocating the communication is part of the fantasy and may lead to much deeper insight into how to improve your sex life and keep each other satisfied.

Bedroom Ideas

There is a wealth of articles in men's and women's magazines about how to keep your lover satisfied, new sex techniques and even the top ten ways to turn on a man. With this kind of readily available information in print and online, finding new ideas for the bedroom isn't difficult for any couple.

Just remember a few basics when planning new ideas, lovemaking techniques or even sexual positions:

* **Comfort levels and zones-** Not everyone is comfortable with a variety of sexual activities. Some people are turned off by some of the sexual activities that may seem very exciting or even desirable to you. Talking with your husband and discovering the comfort level for each of you should allow you to make modifications, and keep you both happy and satisfied.

* **Fitness level-** Some of the new ideas for the bedroom may involve a fairly high standard of both fitness and flexibility. If you or your spouse isn't quite there yet this can be a goal to work towards together. Also, just as with the comfort level, modifying the sexual position or the technique to match your fitness levels can allow you to enjoy the experience without the pain of pulled muscles, bad backs or aching arms or legs.

* **Pace yourself-** If you are entering into a new part of your improved sexual relationship, keep in mind that you don't have to do everything new all at once. There is still time for the old favorite sexual positions and activities; don't forget that they are just as pleasurable as the new and improved techniques you may want to explore.

* **Don't feel pressured-** Lots of couples don't need new techniques or toys; they just need more of an emotional and physical connection than they have had in the past. Don't be pressured to stay up with the latest sex position or technique; rather, try new things or stay with the tried and true. After all, it is your pleasure and satisfaction that counts, not what some editor in a magazine thinks.

Reverse Roles

● ● ● ● ● ● ● ●

A great technique for married couples for spicing up their love life without making any other changes is to try a role reversal. This doesn't mean that the man assumes the role of the woman or vice versa, but it does mean that the more passive member of the couple becomes the sex instigator, while the more sexually aggressive one becomes the passive spouse.

This can be challenging for both people in the marriage since they have to curb their natural behavior when it comes to initiating and responding to sex. The passive spouse -- which can be the man or woman -- needs to take affirmative action to instigate a sexual encounter. This can really build sexual tension and arousal and will give him or her more confidence in signalling sexual desires. The more dominant sexual spouse -- again it can be either spouse -- will then have to be more passive: a complete switch of roles that can be very stimulating.

Role reversals, like all sexual games and techniques, don't have to happen all the time. They can be incorporated into dates, spontaneous sex or planned sexual encounters between the couple.

Things To Consider

As mentioned throughout the book, the more consistently you attend to the sexual relationship you have with your spouse, the stronger it will become. The more you consider and plan for sex, the more often you will have sex, and the better it will be for both of you.

It is important to keep in mind that there are many things that can influence an individual's sex drive, and it is essential that, as a wife, you are sensitive to these possible dips in your love life and not to take it personally. Many things can have a negative impact on sex drive, including:

* Medical conditions

* Grief, depression or mental health issues

* Changes in lifestyle (i.e. smoking cessation programs)

* Loss of a job

* Changes in the family structure

* Moving to a new town or city

* Financial pressures

By working together as spouses, and aside from just focusing on the sexual component of the marriage, you can work together to get back to the love life you both want.

Once you have worked through those issues, you can refocus on connecting sexually and getting your love life back on track. Remember that small steps are the starting point of any change, so don't try to take huge leaps; start with those small, small steps.

Date nights are a great way to start boosting your connection with each other. Add more kissing, touching and flirting, even if you aren't planning on having sex that day or evening. Being more physical throughout the day adds to your anticipation of when you will be together. In addition, it shows love, commitment and support -- all things that are proven to increase self-confidence and sex drive.

Celebrating Your Marriage and Great Sex

● ●

While improving your sex life cannot always be measured on a calendar or a checklist, you should be able to notice some positive changes that are occurring. The more techniques, tips and strategies you use to improve your entire marriage, the better your sex life will be.

Most people mistakenly think that improving your sex life means improving your sexual skills, when in fact the emotional connection, as well as your relationship as a couple, is just as important.

You may notice that you and your husband are more likely to spend additional time together outside the bedroom as well. Your increasingly satisfying physical relationship creates more of a feeling of being a strong couple, working together in all aspects of your life.

Your changing and improving sexual and emotional relationships are cause for celebration. With all your new-found confidence in trying new things and communicating your fantasies, wants and desires, these celebrations are sure to be memorable, pleasurable and ever so much more rewarding for all your hard work.

Take the time to rejoice in how close you feel to each other. This can be a terrific reason for a romantic getaway to celebrate your revitalized sex life. Remember: you don't have to plan anything expensive or elaborate; just the opportunity to get away and enjoy each other will be reward enough!